A Drop of Rain

by Tanya Landman

illustrated by Carys Tait

 CAMBRIDGE UNIVERSITY PRESS

 UCL
Institute of Education

High in the sky there is a cloud.

It grows bigger

and bigger

and bigger ...

... until a drop of rain falls to earth.

Down it falls.

Down, down, down.

It falls past an aeroplane.

It falls past birds.

It falls on a stone mountain.

The drop of rain slides down the rock and into a stream.

The stream runs down the mountain.
It grows bigger and bigger and bigger.

There are tiny frogs and tiny fish and tiny flies.

The stream flows into a river.

There are big fish and big animals that come
to drink the water and cool down in the mud.

There are boats on the river, and bridges over it.

There are buildings on each side that get bigger and bigger and bigger.

The river grows wider and deeper ...

... until the river flows into the sea.

There are enormous boats and enormous fish
and enormous animals.

The sun is hot.

The drop isn't rain any more.

It is water vapour rising up into the sky in the hot air.

14

It is cool in the sky.

The vapour turns back into drops of water.

High in the sky there is a cloud.

It grows bigger

and bigger

and bigger...

... until it rains.

A Drop of Rain • Tanya Landman

Reading notes written by Sue Bodman and Glen Franklin

Using this book

Developing reading comprehension

This is a simple explanation text describing the water cycle in a clear and accessible way. It provides a structure to follow a sequence of events, whilst using a more story-style format to explain the scientific process.

Grammar and sentence structure

- Ellipsis (three small dots) is used to add fluency and expression in reading and to add to the build-up of events.
- Several examples of complex sentences which support development of ideas and can be used to explore impact of word order.

Word meaning and spelling

- Use of comparatives (*'bigger'*, *'wider'*, *'deeper'*) as the raindrop moves on its cumulative journey through the cycle.
- The addition of /er/ on some comparative words requires doubling the consonant (*'big – bigger'*).

Curriculum links

Science - The narrative style of retelling a life cycle could be applied to writing other non-fiction explanatory texts. This playing with the genre features can only really be effective after children are familiar with how explanation texts are structured. Other books in the Cambridge Reading Adventure scheme explore different types of cycles. See, for example, 'Making a Car' (Blue band) and 'How Chocolate is Made' (Turquoise band). Experiments with water vapour, ice and steam will demonstrate the water cycle.

Maths – Ordering of size related to number, linked to ordering of numbers: bigger than ... or smaller than ... a given number.

Literacy – Collect examples of comparative and superlative adjectives. Present on a word wall or in a class dictionary.

Learning Outcomes

Children can:

- read fluently with attention to punctuation
- manage effectively a growing variety of texts, including non-fiction
- make predictions about the content
- read decodable two-syllable words.

A guided reading lesson

Book Introduction

Give each child a book and read the title to them.

Orientation

Activate children's prior experiences of rain and weather patterns. Be sensitive – some children may have had experience of floods or drought.

Give a brief overview of the book, using language structures relevant for explanatory texts.

This book is going to explain something to us. We will learn what happens to a drop of rain when it falls from the sky. This is called the water cycle. Make links with other explanation texts children may have encountered (e.g. life cycles).

Preparation

Page 2: There is some unusual print layout on this page. Check that children can track accurately across the lines of text. Note the use of ellipsis – this occurs again several times during the text (e.g. page 11). Ask: *What do you notice here? This punctuation is called ellipsis. What effect do you think the author wanted to make?*

Clarify what is meant by *'falls to earth'* on this page.